CHICAGO

WHITE SOX

BY DOUGLAS CARL

SportsZone

An Imprint of Abdo Publishing
abdobooks.com

abdobooks.com

Published by Abdo Publishing, a division of ABDO, PO Box 398166, Minneapolis, Minnesota 55439. Copyright © 2023 by Abdo Consulting Group, Inc. International copyrights reserved in all countries. No part of this book may be reproduced in any form without written permission from the publisher. SportsZone™ is a trademark and logo of Abdo Publishing.

Printed in China.
102022
012023

Cover Photo: Cole Burston/Getty Images Sport/Getty Images
Interior Photos: Ron Vesely/Getty Images Sport/Getty Images, 4, 6; Mark Rucker/Transcendental Graphics/Getty Images Sport/Getty Images, 8; Corbis/Corbis Historical/Getty Images, 9; Bain News Service/Interim Archives/Archive Photos/Getty Images, 11; Diamond Images/Getty Images, 12; Bettmann/Getty Images, 14, 21, 25; Transcendental Graphics/Archive Photos/Getty Images, 17; Hulton Archive/Getty Images, 18; Focus on Sport/Getty Images, 22, 28; Paul Natkin/Archive Photos/Getty Images, 26; Owen C. Shaw/Getty Images Sport/Getty Images, 29; Ronald C. Modra/Getty Images Sport/Getty Images, 31; John Reid III/MLB Photos/Getty Images Sport/Getty Images, 32; Ron Vesely/MLB Photos/Getty Images Sport/Getty Images, 35; Brad Mangin/MLB/Getty Images, 36; Rich Pilling/MLB/Getty Images, 38; Alex Trautwig/MLB/Getty Images, 41

Editor: Steph Giedd
Series Designer: Becky Daum

Library of Congress Control Number: 2022940396

Publisher's Cataloging-in-Publication Data

Names: Carl, Douglas, author.
Title: Chicago White Sox / by Douglas Carl
Description: Minneapolis, Minnesota: Abdo Publishing, 2023 | Series: Inside MLB | Includes online resources and index.
Identifiers: ISBN 9781098290139 (lib. bdg.) | ISBN 9781098275334 (ebook)
Subjects: LCSH: Chicago White Sox (Baseball team)--Juvenile literature. | Baseball teams--Juvenile literature. | Professional sports--Juvenile literature. | Sports franchises--Juvenile literature. | Major League Baseball (Organization)--Juvenile literature.
Classification: DDC 796.35764--dc23

CONTENTS

CHAPTER 1

GHOSTS OF THE PAST

In 1989 a famous film came out called *Field of Dreams*. In it, an Iowa farmer builds a baseball field on his land. Magically, players from the 1919 Chicago White Sox emerge from his cornfield and begin playing on the homemade ballpark.

The 1919 White Sox are a legendary team, but not for good reasons. Eight players from the roster were permanently banned from baseball for purposefully losing the World Series. In the hit movie, the players come back to redeem themselves.

The field used in the film is a real place, located just outside of Dyersville, Iowa. Every year, tourists flock there to see the famous ballpark in the cornfield.

Tim Anderson looks to field the ball during the Field of Dreams Game in Dyersville, Iowa, in August 2021.

The White Sox celebrate as Tim Anderson (7) crosses home plate after hitting a walk-off home run in the Field of Dreams Game.

In August 2021, Major League Baseball (MLB) decided to hold a game there. Naturally, the Chicago White Sox were chosen as the home team.

Their opponent was the New York Yankees. The teams played out a tense game in front of close to 8,000 fans. With one out in the bottom of the ninth, the Yankees led 8–7. But Chicago had a runner on and star shortstop Tim Anderson at the plate.

Anderson wasted no time. He swung at the first pitch from Yankees closer Zach Britton, sending it deep into right field for a game-winning home run. The ball sailed over the fence and into the cornfield. Anderson practically danced around the bases before he was mobbed by teammates at home plate. On a field known for its Hollywood roots, the White Sox star had provided a movie-worthy ending.

BORN ON THE SOUTH SIDE

Chicago has been home to baseball stars for well over 100 years. But before the White Sox set up shop on the city's South Side, they were a minor league team in Sioux City, Iowa. In 1893 a man named Charles Comiskey bought the team and moved it to St. Paul, Minnesota. When St. Paul also turned out not to be a good fit, in 1900 Comiskey moved the team southeast to Chicago, where it has been ever since.

Chicago already had one team, of course. The Cubs were original members of the National League (NL). When the White Sox—known at first as the White Stockings—moved to Chicago, they became original members of the American League (AL).

The White Stockings played in the first-ever AL game on April 24, 1901. They defeated Cleveland 8–2 at Chicago's South Side Park. The White Stockings won the AL title that year.

White Sox pitcher Ed Walsh warms up before a 1910 game in Chicago.

And in the days before the World Series, that was that.

THE HITLESS WONDERS

The White Stockings eventually became the White Sox to save space in newspaper headlines. The Sox in those early days were led by a few star players. Pitcher Ed Walsh was the team's ace. His spitball danced its way to home plate and was extremely difficult to hit. Walsh eventually retired with a career earned-run average (ERA) of 1.82, the lowest in MLB history.

The White Sox stars were pitchers because the offense couldn't do much at all. The 1906 team was known as "the Hitless Wonders." They had just a .230 batting average as a team, the worst in the AL.

The White Sox overcame those hitting struggles to win the AL title. Still, few expected them to be a match for the crosstown Cubs in the third-ever World Series. The Cubs had won 116 games, an all-time record.

The White Sox hit even worse in the World Series than they had during the season. But their pitching was excellent. They shut out the Cubs or held them to one run three times. Walsh won both of his starts. The Sox shocked the Cubs and the baseball world by winning the Series in six games.

Slugger "Shoeless Joe" Jackson set a White Sox record with 21 triples in 1916.

A NEW NEIGHBORHOOD

In 1910 the White Sox made West 35th Street their permanent home. White Sox Park, later named Comiskey Park in 1913, opened on July 1 with a sellout crowd. The Sox called the stadium home for the next 80 years.

The White Sox built something special in their new home. "Shoeless Joe" Jackson and Eddie Collins were among the best hitters in baseball. Ray Schalk became a Hall of Fame catcher, and Eddie Cicotte, Lefty Williams, and Red Faber were some

BABE IN CHICAGO?

The Boston Red Sox's sale of Babe Ruth's contract to the New York Yankees in 1919 is known as one of the worst moves in baseball history. But Ruth almost became the home run king in Chicago, not New York. Shortly after losing the World Series, the White Sox submitted the second-highest bid for the slugger, offering $60,000 along with "Shoeless Joe" Jackson. Instead, the Yankees took Boston's $100,000, and the rest is history.

of the best pitchers. In 1917 the White Sox won 100 games for the first time and won the AL title.

In the World Series, Chicago faced the New York Giants. Cicotte, known for his range of tricky pitches, led his team to a win in Game 1. Faber then won Game 2. But both pitchers would lose their next starts.

On just one day of rest, Faber pitched again in Game 5 in relief. He threw two perfect innings as the White Sox came back from a 5–2 deficit to win. Amazingly, Faber then started two days later in Game 6 and allowed just two runs in a complete game. Chicago won 4–2 to capture another World Series title.

THE BLACK SOX

After a sixth-place finish in 1918, nobody knew what to make of the White Sox going into 1919. But they came out on Opening Day and crushed the St. Louis Browns 13–4. Jackson had three hits, and Williams pitched a complete game. That was just the start, as the Sox went on to win the AL title.

White Sox ace Eddie Cicotte led the AL in both wins and complete games in 1919.

Players stand during the National Anthem at a 1963 game at Comiskey Park I, home of the White Sox until 1990.

They faced the Cincinnati Reds in the World Series, which was to be a best-of-nine contest. After delivering a strike on his first pitch, Cicotte, normally one of the best pitchers in the game, hit a batter with his second delivery in Game 1. Problem after problem ensued, and the Reds crushed the White Sox 9–1. They beat another Sox great in Williams in Game 2.

Chicago won Game 3. But a pair of Cicotte errors cost the Sox Game 4. Chicago would force an eighth game, but Williams was unable to get out of the first inning. Cincinnati won 10–5 to take the Series.

The way Chicago lost looked suspicious to some people. There were rumors that White Sox players were paid to lose intentionally so that gamblers could bet on the Reds and win. Comiskey denied the rumors.

Still, an investigation was underway during the fall of the 1920 season. The White Sox played well, winning 96 games and finishing in second place. But the investigation haunted them all year.

Finally in August the following year, the investigation concluded. Throughout the investigation, four White Sox players came forward and admitted that they had done things to lose the World Series on purpose. However, the players were cleared of fault because the documents with their confessions had mysteriously gone missing.

Still, even though the eight players who had participated in the scheme were found innocent, seven of them who were still active were suspended right away, as decided by Kenesaw Mountain Landis, the new MLB commissioner. All eight were later banned from baseball for life. The event became known as the "Black Sox" scandal.

Some, such as Jackson, maintained their innocence. But he and his teammates never played pro baseball again. And it devastated the White Sox for decades to come.

OUT OF THE DARKNESS

The Black Sox scandal did serious damage to the reputation of the White Sox. And it set the team back on the field with the immediate removal of some of its best players. Chicago went from one of the best teams in the AL to one of the worst. From 1921 to 1936, the Sox finished in the top half of the AL just once.

For 30 years after the scandal, the White Sox had only seven winning seasons. The main reason Chicago's fans came to the ballpark was star Luke Appling. The shortstop joined the team in 1930 and played for 20 seasons. Along the way, he set team records for games played, hits, and runs. But in his time with the White Sox, the team never finished higher than third place.

Hall of Famer Luke Appling played his entire career with the White Sox.

RISING AGAIN

Chicago became competitive again under manager Jimmy Dykes in the mid-1930s, coming as close as eight games back of winning the AL in 1940. But it wasn't until the 1950s that the team became a serious contender in the league.

Just as the White Sox said goodbye to Appling in 1951, in came three new stars in pitcher Billy Pierce, second baseman Nellie Fox, and outfielder Minnie Miñoso. All three players ended up having their numbers retired in Chicago. Miñoso and Fox made the Hall of Fame. Miñoso also made Sox history. The native of Cuba was the first Black player for the White Sox.

THE FIRST ALL-STAR GAME

Back in 1933, the All-Star Game was just an idea. Chicago sportswriter Arch Ward came up with the concept. The city wanted to hold a big athletic competition as part of hosting the World's Fair. Ward had the idea to match up the best players in all of baseball against each other. The game was held at Comiskey Park on July 6, 1933. The AL won 4–2. The game was a hit, and it's been played ever since.

THE GO-GO SOX

The 1950s Sox weren't a team of power hitters. The 1959 team was dead last in home runs but first in stolen bases. They earned the nickname "the Go-Go Sox."

Ted Kluszewski only played the 1959 and 1960 seasons with the White Sox, but he made an impact offensively in his time there.

The 1959 season was one of change on the South Side. After nearly six decades in Chicago, the team was no longer controlled by the Comiskey family. Bill Veeck, who had previously owned the Cleveland Indians and St. Louis Browns, took over the team after 1958. Veeck was a master promoter who brought many innovations to the White Sox.

Early Wynn joined the White Sox in 1958 and won the Cy Young Award the next year after winning a league-high 22 games.

After finishing in second place in 1957 and 1958, the White Sox broke through to win the AL pennant in 1959. The addition of slugger Ted Kluszewski during the season was a big boost to the offense. The city celebrated clinching the pennant. Chicago fire commissioner Robert Quinn turned on the city's air-raid sirens, scaring some residents that there was an emergency.

In the first World Series on the South Side in 40 years, the White Sox faced the Los Angeles Dodgers. In Game 1, Early

Wynn and Gerry Staley combined to pitch a shutout and Kluszewski socked two homers as Chicago rolled 11–0. The White Sox built a 2–0 lead in Game 2 but went on to lose. The Dodgers then won the next two to put Chicago on the edge of elimination.

In Game 5, the Dodgers turned to pitcher Sandy Koufax. The future Hall of Famer allowed just a single run, but that was enough as the White Sox forced Game 6. However, Chicago was simply overwhelmed in that game, falling behind 6–0 early and losing 9–3.

CLOSE CALLS

The White Sox had a winning record in each of the next eight years, but they weren't able to capture another pennant. Meanwhile, Veeck was working his magic trying to attract more fans to Comiskey Park. One of his most famous innovations was the "exploding" scoreboard in center field.

Inspired by a pinball machine, the stadium scoreboard would light up and fireworks would go off anytime Chicago hit a home run. Due to poor health, Veeck was forced to sell the Sox after just two years, but the lights and fireworks remained after his departure.

While Chicago didn't win any pennants, they did come close. On September 16, 1964, the White Sox were tied for first place. But three losses in their next four games dropped them back. Despite a nine-game winning streak to finish the season, the team never recovered and missed the pennant by a single game.

The 1967 Sox spent most of the first half of the season in first place. That was despite finishing with the second-worst team batting average in all of MLB. The White Sox were in a battle the rest of the year as a four-team race emerged for the pennant. Going into the last weekend, all four had a shot at the World Series.

Chicago needed a lot of help. The White Sox had to win all their games and hope for other teams to lose. But they lost the series opener 1–0 and were out just like that.

GO, SOX?

Despite their success, the White Sox struggled to draw many fans. They were sixth in the AL in 1967, even though they contended for a pennant all year. In 1968 Chicago began playing some games in Milwaukee. That city to the north had recently lost the Braves to Atlanta and still had plenty of baseball fans.

The games were a hit. The White Sox drew way more fans in the Milwaukee games than they did at Comiskey. They played in Milwaukee again in 1969. The experiment was such a success

White Sox owner Bill Veeck was known for his many stunts to get fans to the ball park. At one game, spacemen arrived in a helicopter to provide pregame entertainment.

that a group from Milwaukee wanted to buy the White Sox and move them there. But the AL killed the deal, and the team stayed in Chicago.

Still, the attendance problem wasn't getting better. Comiskey Park was aging, and the White Sox were rarely competitive. They needed a spark.

THE SOUTH SIDE HITMEN

Moving rumors continued to follow the White Sox. In the 1970s, the team was believed to be on its way west. Seattle had just lost its team in 1969 and was doing whatever it could to get a new one.

But then Dick Allen arrived in the White Sox lineup. The slugger came in a trade with the Los Angeles Dodgers before the 1972 season. Allen was a good player but had some clashes with teammates and management at previous teams.

Free from all of that, Allen swung for the fences and often connected. He blasted 37 homers and drove in 113 runs in his first season on the South Side. That earned him the AL Most Valuable Player (MVP) Award.

Along with RBIs and homers, Dick Allen led the AL with a .420 on-base percentage in his first season with the team in 1972.

Allen led the AL in homers again in 1974. However, he walked away from the team with a few weeks left in the season and was traded to different teams until his retirement in 1977. He had a huge impact in just three seasons with the Sox. He got credit for saving baseball on the South Side, as attendance jumped in his three seasons with the team. Any rumors of the team moving disappeared after that.

VEECK RETURNS

Also helping save the White Sox was Bill Veeck, who repurchased the team in 1975. By then, attendance had fallen to 9,269 fans per game, ranking 11th of 12 teams in the AL. Veeck went to work giving fans a reason besides baseball to come to a ballgame. Veeck's tactics weren't always favorable, but they were mostly effective.

In 1976 Veeck re-signed Minnie Miñoso, even though he was 52 and hadn't played in the majors since 1964. The goal was for Miñoso to say he had played in five decades of pro baseball. Playing in 1976 would make it four. Though he went only 1-for-8 at the plate in three games that season, Veeck signed him again in 1980 to play in his fifth decade. He went 0–2 at the plate, but he completed his goal.

That same year, Veeck introduced a baseball first: short pants. Chicago took the field wearing their normal jersey but

One of Hall of Famer Minnie Miñoso's nicknames was "Mr. White Sox" because he played 12 seasons with the team between 1951 and 1980.

with shorts and high socks. The widely mocked experiment lasted just three games.

What fans appreciated most were Veeck's efforts on the field. With the White Sox struggling to compete, Veeck made a flurry of off-season trades and free-agent signings to try to get better quickly. He targeted players whose contracts would be up soon. Their teams wanted to get something for them in return. These "rental players," such as Oscar Gamble, Richie

Owner Bill Veeck's Disco Demolition Night promotion was successful in bringing fans to the park, but it resulted in damages to the field and the Sox having to forfeit the second game of a doubleheader.

Zisk, and Eric Soderholm, helped the team win 90 games in 1977, but the Sox still fell just short of the playoffs.

DISCO DEMOLITION NIGHT

Not all of Veeck's promotions went well. He and his son Mike, director of promotions for the White Sox, had the idea for "Disco Demolition Night" in 1979. Disco was a style of music that was popular in the 1970s, but not everyone liked it. The idea was to let fans bring their disco albums to a doubleheader and blow up the records in between games.

The promotion was held in conjunction with a Chicago radio station. Because the event was talked about on the radio, a crowd of nearly 50,000 showed up at Comiskey Park. The Sox weren't expecting any more than 35,000.

During the first game, fans repeatedly threw records onto the field. When it came time to blow the records up, the explosion left a huge crater in center field. Fans began pouring onto the grass, and soon the scene was out of control. The White Sox had to forfeit the second game of the doubleheader.

WINNING UGLY

Veeck's ownership didn't last much longer. Fans liked the crazy promotions, but Chicago still had trouble competing on the field. And Veeck didn't have the money to spend as richer teams did. He sold the White Sox in 1981 to a group led by businessman Jerry Reinsdorf.

Reinsdorf wanted to make a big splash as a new owner. Just a few weeks after buying the team, Reinsdorf and the White Sox surprisingly landed free agent catcher Carlton Fisk. Fisk starred in Chicago for the next 13 years as one of the best catchers in baseball history.

The White Sox also got power-hitting outfielder Greg "the Bull" Luzinski from the Philadelphia Phillies. He joined an outfield that included promising youngster Harold Baines.

Catcher Carlton Fisk was a steady presence behind home plate for the White Sox from 1981 to 1993.

Chicago had a young up-and-coming manager in Tony La Russa. Suddenly, the Sox looked ready to compete.

The 1983 White Sox were led by Fisk, Baines, and rookie outfielder Ron Kittle, who won Rookie of the Year with 35 home runs. In the rotation was LaMarr Hoyt, who became the second White Sox player to win the Cy Young Award as the best pitcher in the AL. It all added up to 99 wins and the AL West title.

Many of those 99 wins were scrappy victories. In a stretch of games in which the team won but didn't play well, the Texas Rangers' manager said the Sox were "winning ugly." They embraced the term and made it their rallying cry.

In Chicago's first postseason game in 24 years, Hoyt took the ball for Game 1 of the AL Championship Series (ALCS). He pitched a great game, and the White Sox won 2–1. But that was

LaMarr Hoyt earned a Cy Young Award for his pitching performance leading the majors with 24 wins during the 1983 season.

the only highlight, as the Baltimore Orioles won the next three to take the series.

GOOD GUYS WEAR BLACK

In the late 1980s, the Sox were again rumored to be on the move. Comiskey Park was old and run-down, and the team wanted a replacement. The White Sox were on the brink of moving to Florida when the state agreed on a plan to fund a new stadium. It began going up across 35th Street.

In 1990, the final year of Comiskey Park, some young Sox talent was starting to pay off. Ozzie Guillen manned shortstop. Guillen had been Rookie of the Year in 1985.

Slugger Frank Thomas played first base. Fisk was still there too, at age 42. The Sox were between eight to ten games behind in the AL West running until the season's final days, finishing second in the AL West with a 94–68 record.

During those final days in 1985, the team previewed some new uniforms that officially debuted the following season. For years the White Sox had worn red, white, and blue. Starting in 1991, the team switched to black and silver and brought back an old-fashioned interlocking Sox logo. The uniforms were a hit, and the team's motto became "Good guys wear black." As the Sox moved to their new ballpark across the street, also originally called Comiskey Park, their uniforms were a good-looking tribute to their past.

Thomas turned into a superstar, and in 1993 he was league MVP. Pitcher Jack "Black Jack" McDowell won the Cy Young Award. The White Sox rolled to the AL West title and

HAWK THE GM

Former MLB player Ken "Hawk" Harrelson began broadcasting for the White Sox in 1982. In 1985 he stepped out of the booth to take on a role as the team's general manager. He lasted less than a year and was known for firing manager Tony La Russa, who then went on to a Hall of Fame career managing the Oakland A's and St. Louis Cardinals. Harrelson returned to broadcasting, where he enjoyed an award-winning career until his retirement after the 2018 season.

Jack McDowell led the majors in shutouts and wins in 1993.

faced the Toronto Blue Jays in the ALCS with a trip to the World Series on the line.

McDowell was knocked out in the seventh inning in Game 1, quieting the home crowd as the White Sox lost 7–3. After dropping Game 2, Chicago would rally to take Games 3 and 4. But McDowell lost again in Game 5, and Toronto eliminated the Sox in Game 6.

The Sox were back in a big way in 1994. They were 67–46 and in first place in the new AL Central by August. But that was when a player's strike halted the MLB season. Thomas was named MVP, but the playoffs were canceled. Chicago had to wait a while for another shot.

DON'T STOP BELIEVING

During the late 1990s, the White Sox regularly came close to winning their division only to fall short, finishing second in 1996, 1997, 1998, and 1999. And that was with one of the league's best power hitters in Frank Thomas, who passed Carlton Fisk for the team's all-time home run record in 1996.

Of those close-call teams, the 1997 one had maybe the best shot at a title. Thomas was having an MVP-type season. Ozzie Guillen and third baseman Robin Ventura were at their peaks. The White Sox were three games out of first place on July 31.

Despite all of this, Chicago management decided to trade key players and give up on the season. Fans called it "the white

Frank Thomas emerged as one of baseball's great power hitters during his 16 years with the White Sox from 1990 to 2005.

flag trade." At the end of the season, the White Sox finished six games back in second place.

AIR JORDAN GRABS A BAT

In 1993 Chicago Bulls basketball star Michael Jordan shocked the world by announcing his retirement from basketball. Even more surprising was when he said he was going to pursue a baseball career. The White Sox signed Jordan to a minor league contract in 1994. He went to spring training and spent most of his career playing at the Double-A level, which is two steps below MLB. Jordan struggled to hit, as he hadn't played baseball since his youth, but he did steal 30 bases. After one year in the minors, Jordan returned to basketball and helped the Bulls win three more championships.

It was tough for fans to take at the time. But by 2000, two of the players the White Sox received from those trades were playing big roles for the team. Relief pitchers Bob Howry and Keith Foulke helped the Sox make a surprising run to the playoffs that season. Foulke saved 34 games. The team also had an exciting offense led by Thomas, first baseman Paul Konerko, and outfielder Carlos Lee.

A LEGEND RETURNS

After another second-place finish in 2003, manager Jerry Manuel was fired. In came Guillen, in his first managing job after retiring as a player at the end of the 2000 season. He proved to be the right manager at the right time.

Pitcher Mark Buehrle won 161 games for the White Sox, which ranked sixth in team history when he left as a free agent before the 2012 season.

Some key injuries kept the White Sox in second again in 2004, but they made some big additions for 2005. Lee was traded for outfielder Scott Podsednik. And the team signed free agents such as outfielder Jermaine Dye and catcher A. J. Pierzynski. They also picked up reliever Bobby Jenks from the Los Angeles Angels.

The White Sox pitching rotation was led by Mark Buehrle. The veteran staff also included Jon Garland, José Contreras, and Freddy García. The team's pitching was a strength all season.

The 2005 White Sox won 99 games, their most in a season since 1917. They won the AL Central and looked ahead to

José Contreras winds up against the Houston Astros in Game 1 of the 2005 World Series.

success in the playoffs. As the playoffs rolled around, team leader Pierzynski found a song to inspire them. It was "Don't Stop Believin'" by the band Journey.

A DOMINATING RUN

The White Sox made a statement in their playoff opener over the Boston Red Sox. Pierzynski hit a three-run homer in a five-run first inning. Contreras allowed only two runs as

Chicago went on to win 14–2. The White Sox didn't repeat that offensive performance, but they swept away the Red Sox in three games.

Next up were the Los Angeles Angels with a trip to the World Series on the line. In Game 1, Contreras was nearly as good as he had been against the Red Sox. But the White Sox bats were quiet. The Angels won 3–2. Contreras pitched an impressive 8 1/3 innings. But over the next three games, the rest of the White Sox staff was even better.

In Game 2, Buehrle went all nine innings for a complete game win. Garland did it in Game 3. Then it was García in Game 4. Contreras then finished off the series with a complete game of his own. No team had pitched four complete games in a row in a postseason series since 1956. And the White Sox did it to make their first World Series in 88 years.

PARTY LIKE IT'S 1917

The White Sox kept right on believing as they went into the World Series against the Houston Astros. Game 1 was a tough test against the legendary Roger Clemens. But they knocked Clemens out of the game after two innings on their way to a 5–3 win.

Game 2 was a wild one on the South Side. Houston led 4–2 going into the bottom of the seventh. The Sox loaded the

A.J. Pierzynski rushes pitcher Bobby Jenks after the final out in Game 4 of the 2005 World Series.

bases after Dye was hit by a pitch. Whether he was actually hit wasn't clear. Either way, Konerko came up next and hammered a grand slam. Houston would eventually tie it, only for Podsednik to win it with a homer in the bottom of the ninth.

Chicago fell behind 4–0 early in Game 3. The White Sox rallied to take the lead, but an Astros run in the eighth forced extra innings. Geoff Blum's home run broke a 5–5 tie in the 14th as Chicago eventually won 7–5. Game 4 was the closest one yet. In the eighth inning, Dye drove in the only run of the game with a single. Jenks, who had saved just six games in the regular season, came on for his fourth save of the playoffs.

With two outs in the ninth, Jenks faced Houston's Orlando Palmeiro. The speedy lefty chopped a high, slow bouncer over the mound. Chicago shortstop Juan Uribe chased it down in front of second base, then hustled a quick throw to first. It was barely in time to get the runner. Konerko threw his hands up as the umpire signaled the out. The White Sox mobbed Jenks. After 88 long years, the White Sox were champions again.

REBUILDING

The White Sox could not repeat their surprise success of 2005. It took three more seasons to reach the playoffs. Chicago beat the rival Minnesota Twins in a one-game playoff to win the AL Central in 2008 but quickly lost 3–1 to the Tampa Bay Rays in the AL Division Series (ALDS).

After that, the team came apart. Guillen was released from the team after a losing season in 2011. By 2013 the White Sox were in last place, 30 games behind the division leaders.

By 2017 the White Sox decided to go in a new direction. Top players were traded in exchange for talented young players who could make an impact in a few years. Ace pitcher Chris Sale was traded to the Red Sox for infielder Yoán Moncada and pitcher Michael Kopech. Pitcher José Quintana went to the Chicago Cubs for slugging outfielder Eloy Jimenez and pitcher Dylan Cease. Veteran outfielder Adam Eaton brought back pitcher Lucas Giolito, among others, from the Washington Nationals.

By 2020 all these young players were in the major leagues. They added to a core that already included first baseman José Abreu, who won MVP in 2020, and shortstop Tim Anderson. Giolito tossed a no-hitter in 2020. Abreu was the veteran leader while Anderson was the young up-and-comer. And leading them from the bench was former Sox manager Tony La Russa.

Anderson's exciting playing style won him many fans but also challenged how things were normally done in MLB. Anderson's habit of joyfully tossing his bat after hitting home runs was frowned upon by some,

PITCHING PERFECT

The White Sox had a losing record in 2009, but they experienced one big highlight. Mark Buehrle tossed the second perfect game in White Sox history and just the 18th in MLB history. And he did it at home on the South Side.

Tim Anderson tosses his bat in celebration after hitting a walk-off homer against the Detroit Tigers in 2019.

but many others enjoyed seeing how much fun he had playing the game.

Chicago had some of the greatest young talent in baseball. It led to playoff appearances in 2020 and 2021. That was the first time the White Sox had ever made back-to-back playoffs. The 2020s South Siders just hadn't broken through with a World Series win yet, but fans could see it coming.

TIMELINE

1900

The St. Paul Saints of the Western League move to the South Side of Chicago and become the Chicago White Stockings.

1901

The White Stockings become members of the AL in its first season and win the first league championship.

1906

Despite a reputation as "the Hitless Wonders," the White Sox win the AL for the first time. In a crosstown World Series with the Chicago Cubs, the Sox win in six games.

1910

The White Sox move into Comiskey Park on West 35th Street, which becomes their home for the next 80 years.

1917

Behind star pitcher Eddie Cicotte, the White Sox win the AL again and another World Series, this time in six games over the New York Giants.

1919

The White Sox win the AL again but lose in a surprising upset to the Cincinnati Reds.

1920

An investigation reveals that several Sox players agreed to take money from gamblers to intentionally lose the 1919 World Series. The "Black Sox" scandal results in eight White Sox players being banned from baseball for life.

1922

Charlie Robertson pitches the first perfect game in team history.

1933

Comiskey Park hosts the first MLB All-Star Game.

1959

The "Go-Go Sox" capture the hearts of Chicago with a run to the World Series, but they lose to the Los Angeles Dodgers.

1972

Slugger Dick Allen arrives via a trade and wins the MVP Award in his first season, sparking renewed interest in the White Sox.

1983

The scrappy White Sox make "winning ugly" look good as they capture the AL West title.

1991

The White Sox move across West 35th Street to the new Comiskey Park.

1993

Led by breakout star Frank Thomas, the White Sox win the AL West.

2005

The White Sox advance to the World Series, where they sweep the Houston Astros to win their first championship in 88 years.

2008

The White Sox beat the Minnesota Twins to win the AL Central in front of an all-black-wearing crowd on the South Side.

2021

The White Sox win the AL Central to make the playoffs in back-to-back seasons for the first time ever.

TEAM FACTS

FRANCHISE HISTORY

Chicago White Stockings
(1901–03)
Chicago White Sox (1904–)

WORLD SERIES CHAMPIONSHIPS

1906, 1917, 2005

KEY PLAYERS

José Abreu (2014–)
Tim Anderson (2016–)
Luis Aparicio (1956–62,
1968–70)
Luke Appling (1930–43,
1945–50)
Harold Baines (1980–89,
1996–97, 2000–01)
Mark Buehrle (2000–11)
Eddie Cicotte (1912–20)
Eddie Collins (1915–26)
Red Faber (1914–33)
Carlton Fisk (1981–93)
Nellie Fox (1950–63)
Paul Konerko (1999–2014)
Ted Lyons (1923–42, 1946)

Minnie Miñoso (1951–57,
1960–61, 1964, 1976, 1980)
Billy Pierce (1949–61)
Frank Thomas (1990–2005)
Ed Walsh (1904–16)

KEY MANAGERS

Jimmy Dykes (1934–46)
Ozzie Guillen (2004–11)
Al Lopez (1957–65, 1968–69)

HOME STADIUMS

South Side Park (1900–10)
Comiskey Park I (1910–90)
Also known as:
White Sox Park (1910–13,
1962–75)
Guaranteed Rate Field (1991–)
Also known as:
Comiskey Park II (1991–2002)
U.S. Cellular Field (2003–16)

RED LINE RIVALS

The White Sox and Cubs are connected by the Red Line of Chicago's transit system. The teams never met in the regular season until interleague play started in 1997 but used to play exhibition games against each other regularly.

KEEPING COOL

One of Bill Veeck's many innovations was putting a shower in Comiskey Park for fans to use to cool off on hot summer days. The shower was moved to the new Comiskey Park and is still there.

SOX BEFORE CUBS

Cubs broadcaster Harry Caray made singing during the seventh-inning stretch a tradition at Wrigley Field. But the tradition actually started at Comiskey, where Caray was a broadcaster for 11 years before moving to the North Side.

UNRETIRED

Luis Aparicio's No. 11 jersey is one of many retired by the White Sox. But in 2010, Aparicio himself asked the team to put it back into circulation. His reason was that Chicago had just signed shortstop Omar Vizquel. Both Aparicio and Vizquel came from Venezuela. And because Aparicio respected Vizquel's incredible fielding ability so much, he allowed the new shortstop to wear his number.

GLOSSARY

ace

A team's best starting pitcher.

batting average

A player's number of hits divided by the player's number of at-bats.

contender

A person or team that has a good chance at winning a championship.

earned-run average

A statistic that measures the average number of earned runs that a pitcher gives up per nine innings.

free agent

A player whose rights are not owned by any team.

no-hitter

A complete game in which a team does not allow any hits.

pennant

Another name for a league championship; in MLB, refers to winning either the American or National League.

perfect game

A complete game in which a team retires every opposing batter and allows no base runners.

save

When a relief pitcher comes into a close game and preserves a win.

scandal

An action or event regarded as morally or legally wrong and causing general public outrage.

shut out

Scored no runs.

spitball

A now illegal pitch that uses saliva or some other substance on the ball to make it move in unpredictable ways.

BOOKS

Flynn, Brendan. *The MLB Encyclopedia*. Minneapolis, MN: Abdo Publishing, 2022.

Gitlin, Marty. *MLB*. Minneapolis, MN: Abdo Publishing, 2021.

Hewson, Anthony K. *GOATs of Baseball*. Minneapolis, MN: Abdo Publishing, 2022.

ONLINE RESOURCES

To learn more about the Chicago White Sox, please visit **abdobooklinks.com** or scan this QR code. These links are routinely monitored and updated to provide the most current information available.

INDEX

ABOUT THE AUTHOR

Douglas Carl is a retired English teacher, writer, and lifelong baseball fan.